REFLECTION

REFLECTION

George de Charms

Swedenborg Scientific Association
Bryn Athyn, Pennsylvania

First published as an article in *The New Philosophy*, vol. 107
(January–June 2004), pp. 5–51.

ISBN-13: 978-0-915221-88-2

Typeset by Kirsten Hansen Gyllenhaal
Cover photo by Erland Brock

Swedenborg Scientific Association
P.O. Box 757, Bryn Athyn, PA 19009
Email: ssacontact@verizon.net
www.swedenborg-philosophy.org

Printed in the United States of America

TABLE OF CONTENTS

PREFACE

This study was originally published in *The New Philosophy*, vol. 107 (January–June 2004), pp. 5–51. The journal's late editor, Lennart O. Alfelt, had first received it. Since he entered the spiritual world in 1981 before having an opportunity to publish it, this dates the work to some time in the 1970s perhaps. Nothing on the typescript gives us a firm date.

The typescript was found among material in an archive belonging to the Swedenborg Scientific Association. Neither inquiry of people who may have known something about this series nor a search in *New Church Life* and *The New Philosophy* brought to light any information about its origin.

The author draws on the theological works of Emanuel Swedenborg (1688–1772) published after 1744, the year that can be taken as the turning point when, from devoting his life to scientific and philosophical subjects, Swedenborg began his theological period, which lasted some thirty-eight years. The works written during this period served as a basis for the ideas explored by de Charms. In the text they are referred to in abbreviated form that refers the reader to the following titles: *Spiritual Experiences* (*SE*), *Divine Providence* (*DP*), *Divine Love and Wisdom* (*DLW*), *Arcana Coelestia* (*AC*), *Heaven and Hell* (*HH*), *Conjugial Love* (*CL*), *Doctrine of the Sacred Scripture* (*SS*), and *Apocalypse Revealed* (*AR*). Since all editions have the same section numbers, readers can use any edition to find de Charms' references.

Reference is made in the text to the Swedenborgian view of the spiritual history of mankind. Briefly, this history is defined by three major events: the symbolic Noetic flood which brought the first era of the Most Ancient Church to an end; the first advent of Jehovah as Jesus Christ which at once closed the era of the Ancient Church (that includes the Jewish Church) and ushered in the Christian Church; and the second advent of Jehovah in 1770 by means of the revealing of the internal sense of the Scriptures through the works of Emanuel Swedenborg, (referred to in this text as the "Writings") which opened the present era of the New Church.

NATURE AND IMPORTANCE

"There are more arcana in the doctrine of reflection than in any other whatever." This arresting statement is found in number 733 of the *Spiritual Experiences* by Emanuel Swedenborg. It seems to challenge the generally accepted view, for we have been prone to think of reflection as merely one form, among many, of mental activity. We would ordinarily place it in the same category as sensation, memory, imagination and thought. Why should it contain more arcana than any of these? Are there not other doctrines that are of even greater importance? Consider creation, redemption, and glorification; or influx, providence, and regeneration. Must these not have an even broader application than the doctrine of reflection?

However, when we analyze the teaching of the Writings on the subject of reflection, we learn that it has a universal application because it underlies all the other operations of the human mind. All consciousness depends upon it. Without it there can be no sensation, memory, imagination, or thought. Without it the Lord could not have effected the glorification of His Human, nor could He have provided for the regeneration of man and the salvation of the human race. Not only does it contain the key to the understanding of all the conscious activities of the human mind, but it explains all the countless phenomena of the spiritual world. The life of man on earth is distinguished from that of angels and spirits solely by the fact that they have distinctly different planes of reflection. Because of this, the inhabitants of one world can be completely unconscious of those in the other world, and at the same time can be in constant and intimate association with them. Without this association there could be no conscious life in either world. Open communication between the two worlds is made possible only by bringing both men and spirits temporarily into a state of reflection that is common to both.

Furthermore, the doctrine of reflection has never been revealed before in the entire history of the human race. The laws of reflection have indeed been operative from the beginning of time, but they have not been known. Men have enjoyed the benefits of their operation and have taken them for granted without even trying to understand them. Just as the laws of gravity existed before the time of Newton, and those of electricity before Franklin began to investigate them, so the laws of reflection were operative before they were revealed in the Writings of the Lord's second coming. They were unknown to the men of the Most Ancient Church who nevertheless had great heavenly wisdom. They were concealed from the men of the Ancient Church even in the days of its pristine glory. They could not be made known to those who belonged to the Jewish Church, nor even to the Christian Church before the Lord had made His second coming. Only through the medium of one who could live consciously in both worlds at the same time, and who therefore could compare the two worlds and note how each was related to the other, could the laws of reflection be made known.

These laws are now laid open by the Lord because some understanding of them is vital to the establishment of the New Church. Indeed the whole purpose of the Lord's advent was that His heavenly kingdom may be established on the earth. By this is meant a kingdom of heavenly uses in which men may have a greater measure of responsibility and a greater sense of participation than was ever possible before. Being enabled to perform spiritual uses, men can receive the Lord's life in greater fullness and with deeper enjoyment; wherefore the Lord said to His disciples: "I am come that they may have life, and that they may have it more abundantly" (John 10:10). The ability to perform any use depends upon a knowledge and understanding of the laws that are applicable to it. Only the knowledge of spiritual laws can open the way to the performance of spiritual uses. The doctrine of reflection has been revealed to the end that men may be introduced to a whole new realm of spiritual uses, together with the joy of accomplishment that this makes possible.

But what do we mean by "reflection"? The root meaning of the word "reflect" is to bend back. It refers to the bending back of any force that strikes upon a resisting object. Thus light is reflected from a mirror. Similarly in regard to the things of the mind. A stream of sense impulses is passing through the mind every waking moment. Only when this stream is arrested at some point, that is, when one pays attention to it, is it "bent back" or "reflected." Then for the first time does it produce a conscious sensation. We are said to "look" at something because it "strikes our fancy." We perceive it as something that has an important relation to our life, as something that gives either pleasure or pain. For this reason we "take an interest" in it, and are said to "reflect upon it." Thousands of sense impulses pass by unheeded; but whatever we reflect upon is perceived and felt. We become aware of it. The impulses to which we do not pay attention nevertheless make an impression upon the mind and are stored up in the interior memory, producing there an unconscious background out of which new sensations may arise; but the mental world in which we live is made up of a selected strand of sense impulses to which we pay attention, upon which we reflect, and of which therefore we become conscious.

The focus of attention varies with every one according to the love that is active in the mind at any particular time. For this reason the same experience will make a different impression upon different people. One will "see" what another passes by unnoticed. For this reason two people may derive from the same environment very different ideas, and thus may live in different mental worlds.

Not only human beings, but animals also can reflect. They instinctively pay attention to the things in their environment that have relation to their life. They recognize their own food and distinguish it from whatever would be injurious to their health. They know how to avoid their enemies and how to protect their young. They can remember and recall sensations or experiences that are important to their life. They seek what is needful and avoid what is hurtful. All this they do spontaneously without knowing why. But they cannot reflect upon themselves; that is, upon what takes place within their own mind. They are impelled by a single love which is their whole life, and this love dictates all their conscious sensations.

Human beings, on the other hand, are capable of being influenced by various loves or affections. They therefore can see things differently at different times or in different states of mind. While seeing an experience in one state of mind, they can still remember how it appeared under the influence of another affection. They can compare these two divergent impressions and so can decide which they will retain as true and which they will reject. Thus they can reflect not only upon material objects but also upon ideas, and can analyze the nature and quality of their own thoughts. Thus they have a plane of reflection that animals do not possess—a plane whereby they know themselves or become aware of the various loves by which they are moved at different times; and because of this they can choose the loves that are to qualify their life and thus can determine their own character. In this ability lies the moral and spiritual freedom that distinguishes them from the animal creation and makes them human. That is what enables man to become aware of spiritual things and thus to live in a spiritual world. It is the secret of his immortality.

All conscious life is the product of reflection, but human consciousness is the product of spiritual reflection; that is, reflection upon the nature and quality of human life itself, its origin, its inner content, its relation, not only to the world of material objects but also to love itself, and thus to God. Of this, man becomes aware from the teaching of the Word concerning God; that is, concerning the essential quality of love and wisdom. Of this no man would become aware merely by reflecting upon his own inner feelings. These appear to arise within himself. He perceives them only as to their effects. He cannot know, apart from the teaching of the Word, that they inflow from the Lord through the spiritual world and thus through angels and spirits in that world. Their origin is not in man but outside of him; and only when this is realized can man understand that they are not inevitable. Man has the power to determine which of them he will make his own and which he will reject. This no one could possibly know except by reflection upon the teaching of the Word.

Man was endowed from creation with the faculty of spiritual reflection. As soon as man became capable of exercising this faculty, the human soul because immortal. Before this time it could hardly be said that "man" existed, except perhaps in potency. The fetus in the womb may be said to be "human" because of the human life in the seed that progressively builds the body of a potential man. But the fetus has no power of reflection and therefore has no conscious life either on earth or in the spiritual world. It is not the body but the mind that makes the man. Without reflection there is no conscious mind, no awareness of life, no enjoyment of human qualities and attributes; that is, of love and wisdom which are the essential human.

These qualities can be acquired only after birth, and even then, only by slow degrees. Reflection begins with an infant by his noticing most general sensations—the contrast between light and shade, outline and what lies beyond, rough and smooth, loud and soft, and so forth. This is the first plane of consciousness. Only after innumerable such sensations have been perceived and stored in the memory can the infant begin to recognize the relation of various sensations to one another and so to discover "things." Then for the first time does the infant begin to picture things in the imagination and identify these mental pictures with names. He begins to ask "what" things are and to reflect upon the combinations of many isolated sensations. Later the young child discovers what things do, what they are for, and how they can be used. When he begins to reflect upon this he no longer is satisfied to discover things and call them by name. He wants a story about them. He wants to know what they do and why they do it. Here again is a new plane of reflection that opens before the child a vast new world to be explored. As he grows older he begins to recognize abstract ideas, qualities of immaterial or spiritual things, things moral and philosophical, thoughts, truths, and affections or loves. Such are the stages of mental growth from infancy to adult age, and for this reason reflection upon spiritual things is not possible in childhood.

The same law of mental development applies to the race. The first men achieved spiritual wisdom but only by reflecting upon sensations. They perceived spiritual truths within the superficial appearances of nature, the shapes and colors of objects, the sounds of wind and wave, the contrast of light and darkness, of day and night. A study of what is involved in this kind of reflection would throw a flood of light upon the nature and mental quality of that most ancient wisdom as contrasted with the wisdom that is common to man in modern times.

In the Ancient Church, reflection was centered upon knowledges drawn from the Word, from which arose the science of correspondences. Theirs was a different kind of wisdom, concerning which, perhaps we can have a somewhat better idea because it is something we also can experience. Yet unlike ourselves, those ancient people had no regard to scientific facts, to historic accuracy, but only to a parable, a story with a meaning.

When the Lord came into the world, He introduced his disciples to still another plane of reflection; namely, of abstract ideas and their importance to man's spiritual life. He introduced not only the parable, but also the doctrinal sermon, and this became the chief focus of Christian worship. Such doctrine was the expression of a love, an affection, an emotion, rather than an intellectual understanding. That is why such irrational doctrines could be accepted on faith without understanding—the doctrine of a God in three persons, the doctrine of original sin and a vicarious atonement, the doctrine of the resurrection of the body, and many others.

Not until the second coming of the Lord could man be given to reflect even upon reflection itself, and thus to understand spiritual things rationally, and so "enter intellectually into the mysteries of faith." Again a whole new world is presented for exploration—a world of spiritual use, of participation with the Lord in His divine work of salvation, together with a sense of accomplishment and enjoyment never possible before. Because this new plane of reflection is of such vital importance to the establishment of the New

Church, we have been moved to search out from the Writings the doctrine of reflection which alone brings that plane within the reach of human minds, and opens up a limitless opportunity for the establishment, by gradual stages, of the Lord's promised kingdom on earth.

REFLECTION AND HUMAN FREEDOM

The very essence of human life consists of the two faculties called liberty and rationality, and both of these depend for their operation entirely upon man's ability to reflect. It is obvious, of course, that human freedom is by no means absolute. It is limited by many circumstances over which man has no control. No one, for instance, can choose his parents or his ancestors, although he derives from them hereditary tendencies that profoundly affect his life. He has no choice over the time or the place of his birth, and yet racial, national, and family customs play an enormous part in determining what every one thinks and feels. The times under which one grows up— times of peace or war, of economic prosperity or depression—may place many restrictions on one's opportunity to achieve the goals one might desire. Human freedom, therefore, does not imply an unlimited choice, but merely a choice between possible alternatives. This freedom may be enjoyed at times by all men regardless of external circumstances. Yet even this choice is real only so far as it is the result of rational judgment based upon reflection. If, when one is confronted by several alternatives, he merely yields unthinkingly to the one that seems to be the most desirable at the moment, he cannot be said to make a free choice. His action then is preconditioned by some natural impulse, by previous experience, or by instruction and education. This is the case with the great majority of human choices. They can be traced to some prior cause, and for this reason many scientific psychologists are led to believe that man has no choice that is really free. This is certainly true of children, whose behavior is determined either by their native disposition, by whatever emotion happens to be strongest at any given time, or by habits that have been acquired under the influence of parents and teachers. It cannot be otherwise before they have learned how to think; that is, how to reflect and judge for themselves. It is well recognized that no choice can be free unless it is based upon rational judgment. For this reason no one is held responsible under the law before he becomes adult. Even in adult age, no one can be blamed for what he does under the stress of extreme pain or fear or any overpowering passion.

It should be noted that the ability to reflect is progressive. It begins in earliest infancy by reflection upon very general sensations—the contrast between light and shade, smooth and rough, light and heavy, round and square. Gradually one becomes aware of boundaries with spaces in between, of strongly contrasting colors, and by degrees one learns to notice more particular distinctions. Only after innumerable sensations have been stored in the memory can one begin to realize how they are related to one another. One must see objects, feel them, and note their qualities from many different angles before one can even begin to understand "what" they are. Thousands of isolated sensations must be ordered by the mind to form the idea of a "thing." Only then can it be pictured in the imagination, remembered, and recalled even when the object is not present. Only then can one ask for it by name. All this results from noticing how all sensations are intimately related to one another. By this kind of reflection, an ever-increasing number of mental pictures called "things" are built up, producing a whole world of marvels to be explored. But even then, one will not understand what these things really mean until he begins to reflect upon what they do; only then can he realize what they are for, and how they can be used, and this requires a higher kind of reflection which opens up a new and unlimited field of exploration. Such are the successive stages by which the mind of every infant grows.

There can be no rational judgment without knowledge, and all knowledge must be derived, in the last analysis, from bodily sensation. Furthermore, sound judgment requires a sufficiency of accurate knowledge. No choice that is truly free can be based on ignorance or on incorrect data. Nor can a choice be free that is not based upon a genuine sense of values, that is, a sense of what is really most desirable because it will promote the greatest good. Without this even the most accurate knowledge may be used for an unworthy purpose. To do this is an abuse of free choice that can result only in human bondage because it causes man to act contrary to the laws of nature and contrary to the laws of God. What the laws of nature are no one can learn without subordinating his own opinions to the test of experience, and what the law of God is, no one can realize without submitting his mind to the teaching of Divine revelation. That is why the Lord said to "those Jews who believed on Him, If ye continue in My Word, then are ye My disciples indeed, and ye shall know the truth, and the truth shall make you free" (John 8:31, 32).

All children begin with the idea that freedom consists in the ability to do whatever one pleases. They look forward eagerly to growing up in order that they may be liberated from the bond of obedience to parents and teachers and may come into this kind of absolute freedom. Only by slow degrees can they learn that there are laws which no one may successfully defy. The laws of nature are inscribed by the Divine Creator on all things of the material world; and the laws of spiritual life, as revealed in the Word, determine irrevocably the relation of human beings to one another and to the Lord. All freedom arises from willing obedience to these laws; nor can any one obey them willingly unless he knows them and freely chooses, from rational judgment, to follow them. In doing so man achieves a true sense of freedom in which there is fullness of joy and blessing. This is the secret of human happiness. Wherefore it is written: "The judgments of the Lord are true and righteous altogether . . . in keeping them is great reward" (Psalm 19:9, 11).

The Writings, therefore, make a clear distinction between apparent freedom and real freedom, showing that this latter can be attained only through the knowledge, the acknowledgment, and the rational understanding of truth, and this depends entirely upon reflection.

Rational reflection is a distinctly human faculty. By this man is distinguished from the animal creation, as we have already pointed out. Animals reflect upon sensations as affecting their bodily life either for good or ill. They react to them spontaneously, not knowing why. They can have no concept of "things" but only of sensations that satisfy physical needs, longings, and appetites or that give pain and warning of danger to their life. After all, the concept of a "thing" is an abstraction made possible by reflecting upon relations. Of this, animals are incapable because their whole life is dominated by a corporeal love, the love of the body and its life. Man alone is endowed with a love that makes him sensitive to things immaterial and spiritual. He has a soul by virtue of which he is able to live consciously in a spiritual world, sensing the objects of that world even as animals sense the objects of nature. He has an inner mind whence to look down upon his physical sensations, perceive their relations to one another, their true quality, and the use for which they are intended. That is what is meant in Genesis, where it is written: "The Lord God planted a garden eastward in Eden; and there He put the man whom He had formed . . . to dress it and keep it" (Genesis 2:8, 15). In this garden there were two trees, the "tree of life" and the "tree of the knowledge of good and evil." By the "tree of life" is meant the perception of things heavenly and Divine; and by the "tree of the knowledge of good and evil" is meant the perception of things worldly and corporeal. The "tree of life" represents a mind formed by love to the Lord and charity toward the neighbor, while the "tree of the knowledge of good and evil" represents a mind formed by the pleasures of the body and of the world. This latter is called the "animus," which is a mind that man has in common with animals, but the former is called the "mens," an inner mind that is strictly human and belongs to man alone. It is called a "rational" mind because by means of it man can reflect upon relationships, can deduce reasons, and can perceive uses. He can sense higher values whence comes a conscience whereby to govern and control his animal nature that it may serve and promote the ends of a spiritual love. Concerning this ability we read in *Divine Providence* 75:

> Man has not only the affection of natural love but also the affection of spiritual and . . . [celestial] love. For the human mind is of three degrees . . . Wherefore a man can be raised from natural knowledge into spiritual intelligence, and from this into . . . [celes-

tial] wisdom; and from these two, intelligence and wisdom, he can look to the Lord, and thus be conjoined with Him, by which means he lives forever. But as to the affection there would not be this elevation unless man had from rationality [the] ability to elevate the understanding, and from liberty, [the] ability to wish to do so. By means of these two faculties . . . [man] is able to reflect within himself upon the things which he perceives . . . through the bodily senses; and he can also think above concerning what he is thinking below. For any one can say, I have thought this, and I think this. Also, this I have willed, and this I will; or again, I understand this, that it is so, and I love this because it is such; and so on. Thus it is manifest that a man can think above the thought, seeing it as beneath him. This ability a man has from rationality and from liberty, from rationality that he can think higher, and from liberty, that from affection he wills to think so; for unless he had liberty so to think, he would not have the will, and thus not [have] the thought. Wherefore they who do not wish to understand anything but what is of the world and its nature—not even what moral and spiritual good and truth are—cannot be raised from knowledge into intelligence, still less into wisdom, for they have blocked up these faculties. They therefore make themselves men only in being able to understand, if they wish, and in being able to wish, from the rationality and liberty implanted in them. From these two faculties one is able to think and to speak from the thought. In all other things they are not men, but beasts; and some, from the abuse of these faculties, are worse than beasts.

The knowledge of things both spiritual and natural must enter the mind by way of the bodily senses. For this reason the Word must be given in forms that can be sensually perceived, and primarily through sight and hearing. In ancient times it had to be spoken by the prophets in words that men could hear and understand, or it had to be written by them in books that men could read. It was spoken by the Lord Himself when He was in the world and was perpetuated by the inspired writings of the Evangelists. Finally, it was imparted in rational language that lays open the deeper meaning of the Scripture through the Writings of Emanuel Swedenborg. By this means there is imparted to man a vision of God and a perception of His Divine and Infinite qualities which could not be transmitted by nature alone. Nature is so vast, so complex, so apparently self-sufficient, that man cannot penetrate its superficial appearances to perceive the divine life within it. In the Word, the objects of nature are selected, arranged, and ordered into a simplified form through which the Divine may in some measure be seen. This becomes more and more evident as man reflects upon the teaching of the Word from a love that has been insinuated into his mind especially during infancy and childhood by influx out of heaven. Thence comes the desire to know and understand what the Word teaches. It causes man to reflect upon it and thus to become aware of its deeper meaning. By this mode alone does man come to know the laws of God, that he may reflect upon them, and learn, in increasing measure, to understand them and take delight in them. From this comes genuine freedom—freedom, that is, to choose between the promptings of the animus or external mind and those of the mens or internal mind. This choice is possible only so far as the teaching of the Word is known that it may be compared to the outward appearances of nature, and so far as man freely, as a result of rational reflection, adopts the teaching of the Word as the law of his life. This is the key to a truly religious life. Everyone must learn the truth of the Word by his personal reading and reflection that he may accept it, not on the testimony of others, but because the Lord Himself has said it and because the man himself understands it and acknowledges it to be the truth. Then for the first time can the Lord, from his conscience, direct his judgment and lead him in the way to true freedom and everlasting happiness.

THE PLANE OF REFLECTION DETERMINES THE OBJECTIVE WORLD IN WHICH WE LIVE

We have stated that conscious life can result only when the forces of the spiritual world interact with the forces of the material world. The constant stream of sense impulses striking upon the cerebrum makes no distinct or meaningful impression upon the mind unless its flow is checked by some love that affects the mind from the spiritual world. That is what causes one to notice, to pay attention, and thus to become aware. The reason is that, regarded in themselves, sense impulses have no meaning. They enter haphazardly through sight, hearing, taste, smell, and touch in a confused and disordered stream of separate and unrelated impressions. They may be compared to flotsam and jetsam washed up by the tide. Yet they are the only materials out of which any idea of shape, or form, or tangible substance may be produced in the mind. Love selects from them whatever is in accord with its purpose and orders it to form a mental picture that has significance. It is perceived either as delightful or undelightful, as something that imparts pleasure or pain. It is felt either as accordant with the life of man's love or as injurious to it. Sense impulses therefore provide the material out of which form is produced, while love brings scattered parts into mutual relationship and reveals their quality, that is, their use. This perception of quality is what causes the mind to notice and thus to become conscious.

Love therefore produces reflection. It reaches out to hold and to increase any sensation that is delightful, and shrinks from what is perceived as painful and tries to escape from it. This spontaneous reaction is what we call the will; and the form that pictures it in the mind is called the understanding. These two combine to produce conscious life, and without them both no consciousness is possible.

This applies to animals as well as to human beings. The soul of every animal is a love which enables him to perceive the quality of sensations that impinge upon him from his material environment. It causes him to feel sensations either as pleasant or unpleasant and thus to become aware of their relation to his physical life. However, he cannot reflect upon the quality of his love. That is because he is moved by only one love and cannot compare it with other affections. Human beings, on the other hand, are affected by various loves. They can compare them and note their differences. They can distinguish between loves that are conducive to their well-being and happiness and those that are not. They therefore can reflect upon the quality of spiritual forces and can picture them in the form of spiritual ideas. That is why men can become conscious of a spiritual world and can perceive what are called human values. Reflecting upon these things, man can become aware of deeper longings, of delights which physical pleasures do not satisfy. This is possible because man, unlike animals, is endowed with an inner mind sensitive to the forces and the objects of a spiritual world and is capable of perceiving their relation to his life.

Because consciousness requires the interaction between two worlds, man may be said to live in both worlds at the same time. Indeed, the spiritual world and the natural world are so intimately associated that the one cannot exist without the other. That is because the spiritual world is a world of causes, and the natural world is a world of effects. There can be no effect without a cause and no cause without an effect. For this reason there cannot be two separate worlds, each existing by itself. There can be only a dual world composed of two constantly interacting parts. For the same reason man cannot have two separate minds, one wholly sensual and natural and the other purely spiritual. He must have two distinctly different organs of sensation, one sensitive to spiritual forces and the other sensitive to material forces, but these can produce no mental consciousness except as they act in concert.

Why then is it, we may well ask, that man, to all appearance, lives for a time in the natural world, being altogether oblivious of his spiritual environment and then, when the body dies, awakens to all the wonders of the spiritual world while becoming altogether oblivious of things natural and material? It is indeed a remarkable provision of the Divine Providence that men on earth live solely in their own world, and spirits, after death, similarly live in theirs, in spite of the fact that both are under the constant influence of both worlds. This can be true only because in each world conscious life is determined by the plane on which reflection takes place.

During his life on earth, man is so dependent upon physical sensation that he cannot think apart from space and time. His love, and therefore his attention, are focused upon the needs of the body and the natural world. He can conceive of what is spiritual only in relation to these things. He feels affections as if they originated within himself and can conceive of them only as abstractions. He may learn from revelation that he is constantly being influenced by spirits and angels, but this is a matter of knowledge, not of sensible experience. For this reason he is unaware of his spiritual environment, and he cannot visualize the spiritual world as existing outside of himself except in terns of space and time. The chief reason why this is so is that all sensation comes to him by way of the material body and its organs of sensation. The body may be compared to a glove through which all sensation must pass and by which the sensation is rendered vague, general, and imperfect. As long as one is in the body he can reflect only upon what he feels through this gross covering. He can be aware of nothing else. Indeed, he cannot even imagine how keen and how delightful sensation would be if this covering were removed. Consider how limited is the range of our sense organs. The eye responds only to those light waves that lie within the spectrum, although there are indefinite extensions of these waves beyond what we know as red light in one direction and what is called violet light in the other. So also the human ear is sensitive to only a few of the sound vibrations that fill the air around us, and even these must be of a sufficient intensity to be heard. So also with taste, smell, and touch, all of which function only within a limited range and remain oblivious to whatever lies beyond. It is true that sight may be considerably expanded by mechanical means by the use of the microscope or the telescope. The ability to hear may be increased by electrical aids. All one's senses may be perfected by training and experience. But still much remains beyond the horizon of our perception. Consider also how the normal function of our sense organs may be impaired by accident or disease, which in extreme cases shuts out all sensation.

Nevertheless, during his life on earth, man can enjoy no physical sensation apart from love, and after death he can enjoy no spiritual sensation apart from the memory of bodily sensation. Every impulse that has reached the brain, whether it has been consciously perceived or not, is retained in the interior memory and becomes the basis for all ideas of form or shape possible to the spirit in the after life. Furthermore, after the death of the body the spirit remains in constant communication with the world of nature, not immediately, but through the minds of men still living on earth. Whatever men picture in the imagination affects the spirits who are associated with them, performing for them the same function that physical sensation performs for man on earth. For this reason it is said that "heaven rests upon the human race as upon its foundation." If the race on earth should perish, or if the bond of communication between the two worlds should in any way be broken, the angels and spirits would become unconscious as if in a swoon. And it is equally true that if men on earth were cut off from all influx from spirits and angels they would be moved by no love, no desire or interest, and would, in consequence, become unconscious.

The restriction imposed by the material body affects not only the ability to feel material objects, but also the ability to perceive spiritual things. We can respond to affections and thoughts only according to states of both body and mind. We experience moods of sadness or of elation for no discernible reason, and these qualify all our conscious life. Because our plane of reflection is in the natural world, we imagine that material things are the source of our happiness, and therefore we labor constantly to amass worldly possessions. Only by degrees can we learn to distinguish between what is spiritual and what is natural. We may learn of the existence of God, of heaven, and of truly human qualities as distinct from the things of earth, but at first we perceive this only as abstract knowledge. We continually gravitate to the delight of external sensations, and because we have to struggle to grasp the delight of heavenly things, the effort to do so cannot be long maintained. Yet the Lord, through the angels, and directly by the teaching of His Word, constantly stirs within us a sense of love to Him, of charity toward the neighbor, of delight in use. By these means He repeatedly calls to us, even as He called to Abram, so long ago, saying: "Get thee out of thy country, and from thy kindred, and from thy father's house, unto a land that I will show thee; and I will make thee a great nation, and I will bless thee, and make thy name great, and thou shalt be a blessing" (Genesis 12:1, 2).

This is a call to withdraw the mind from the constant stream of bodily sensations and from dependence upon ideas of space and time that we may become aware of the qualities of love and wisdom, which at first appear only as abstract and intangible entities. This is essential if we are to acquire any concept of the difference between right and wrong, good and evil, truth and falsity. In no other way can we be gifted with a conscience whereby to form our character. Nevertheless, as long as we are on earth, we do not normally reflect upon these spiritual things. The needs and desires of the body are so immediate and so pressing that we cannot ignore them. They take precedence over the needs of the spirit. Try as we may we cannot think for long apart from them, and for this reason we cannot reflect while in the body as we will be able to reflect after the body has been laid aside. We can indeed elevate our minds "almost into the light in which the angels are," and so doing from time to time we can catch a glimpse of heavenly joys that we may learn to strive for them.

"Man," we read, "so long as he lives in the world . . . cannot be elevated into very wisdom, such as the angels have, but only into higher light, even up to angels, and can receive enlightenment from their light, that flows in from within and illuminates . . . The natural mind may be raised up into the light of heaven in which angels are, and may [thus] perceive naturally, thus not so fully, what the angels perceive spiritually; nevertheless, man's natural mind cannot be raised into angelic light itself" (*DLW* 256, 257). The reason is that while he is on earth, man cannot reflect apart from his material environment. He cannot wholly remove from his mind ideas of space and time. He therefore cannot visualize a spiritual world as existing outside of himself and as consisting of visible, tangible forces and objects without ascribing to these the properties of matter. Although he is being influenced by loves and is capable of forming abstract ideas of human qualities, he remains completely oblivious to the world in which spirits and angels live.

THE VALUE AND IMPORTANCE OF
A FIXED ENVIRONMENT

We have pointed out that during his life on earth all man's conscious sensations come to him through the material body which is like a glove that covers the spirit. To this rule we must note certain exceptions. There may be a partial and temporary removal of this covering while man is still living in the body. This was the case with the ancient prophets when they were in a state of spiritual vision or in dreams. At such times, the life of the body was as it were suspended. The mind was withdrawn from reflection upon physical sensations and focused upon the impulses that come from the spiritual world. The prophet became aware of his spiritual environment and was brought into open communication with spirits and angels. He "saw a vision, he heard a voice, or he dreamed a dream." His personal will was quiescent, and he was swept along by the current of spiritual affections that impinged upon the internal mind. Because the individual will was quiescent, the Lord could move him to see, to feel, and to say things far beyond his comprehension so that he might become a medium for the giving of the Divine Word. This, however, is not a normal state of life but one that is induced from time to time under the immediate control of the Divine Providence.

The two worlds are so intimately interrelated that such an opening of the spiritual sight is possible, and it may take place in varying degrees in order to meet some specific need. It produces the experience of what men call extrasensory perception, of which there is unquestionable evidence, although it may often be confused with pure imagination, with ordinary dreams, or with deliberate pretense of spiritual insight for the sake of some selfish purpose. It is so important for men on earth to live as if in a purely natural world and for spirits and angels to live as if in a purely spiritual world that any deliberate attempt to penetrate the veil is said to be contrary to order. Warning against this is given because it can be destructive of all free choice and rationality without which regeneration is not possible.

Whatever one perceives through the glove of physical sensation is necessarily vague and general. When this covering is removed, one enjoys far keener sensations and perceptions that are incomparably more delightful. Particulars become clear that had been sensed only as a confused mass without distinctions. What has been seen, as it were through a mist, becomes sharply defined. The fact that this is impossible as long as man lives in the body appears indeed as a great disadvantage, yet it is a very important necessity and is compensated for by the fact that on earth man is surrounded by a fixed environment. By means of sense organs and the connecting system of nerves, the mind is brought into contact with the material creation. In no other way can man be given the opportunity of free choice on which depends the formation of human character.

Because of this, men on earth enjoy a kind of freedom quite different from that of spirits and angels. In order to progress from place to place there must be ground on which to walk, propellers by which to move through water or air, or some form of jet propulsion by which to explore outer space. There must be something hard, solid, resistant, to react against. No one can lift himself by his bootstraps. He must be able to lay hold of something outside of himself. This is just as true of the mind as it is of the body. One's state of mind cannot be changed except by contact with something fixed outside of itself. There must be facts which are dependable and at the same time independent of any individual opinion. There must be principles on which one may rely with certainty from which to reason. There must be truth which transcends reason—truth which is self-evident or axiomatic, from which to think. The foundation of all natural knowledge and intelligence is the world of nature, and the foundation of all spiritual intelligence and wisdom is the Word of Divine revelation. These are called the "two foundations of truth" because they are fixed and unalterable and because they exist independently of the human mind as something the mind may lay hold upon to progress, to change its state, to determine its character.

The purpose of man's life on earth is that he may freely choose what he will love above all things, and what, from love, he will think and believe. To this end he is presented with alternatives and finds it necessary to accept one in preference to the other. Every action he takes of his own will involves such a choice. No one can go in two different directions at the same time. If he moves at all he must adopt one way and reject the other. As he does this persistently he establishes habits of both will and thought, as a result of which the choice becomes progressively easier, more spontaneous, and effortless. It becomes natural to him and so is appropriated as his own or as his very life. When such a choice has been made and confirmed by living experience, it remains, not because it could not be changed, but solely because there is no will or desire to change it. So far as this is the case, man's character has been fixed to eternity because even the Lord will not compel him to change against his will. To do so would destroy his individuality, in the exercise of which all the joy of life resides. One who has made such a choice on earth has irrevocably determined his place in the spiritual world, whether it be in heaven or in hell, and that is why it is said, "As the tree falls, so shall it lie." Whatever love man has adopted may be perfected to eternity, but it cannot be changed or replaced by any other love.

Every one is confronted by many alternatives during the course of his natural life, but there is one fundamental choice that embraces and determines the character of all the others. It is this: will he claim his life as his own to do with as he pleases, or will he acknowledge that it is a gift from God to be used in accord with the Lord's will rather than his own? No one of sound mind who reaches adult age can avoid making this decision, at least in some degree. He must decide to act in accord with his conscience or against it, and this whether his conscience is true or false. By a conscience here is meant whatever he has come to believe is right because it is decreed by God. One who persistently strives to obey his conscience is said to be "innocent" because he is willing to be led and taught, and such a one, however ignorant or mistaken he may be, will come at last into heaven. Such is the universal mercy and loving kindness of the

Lord. Only those who have persisted in self-will during their life on earth will find the gates of heaven closed against them in the other life, but only because they refuse to enter and deliberately choose the life of hell.

Although those who die in infancy and childhood cannot make such a choice, they still can be prepared for heaven in the other life because they are innocent and have not confirmed themselves against the Lord's leading. They can be educated by the angels, and when they reach mature age they can be introduced into the world of spirits where they come in contact with evil spirits and can learn to resist temptation and so make the life of heaven their own by individual choice.

What produces free choice is a love. This causes one to reflect, that is to notice, to pay attention. There constantly pours in upon the mind a stream of sensations or impulses, all of which are transmitted to the brain by the nerves and there knock upon the door of the mind. For the most part this knocking is unheeded and therefore produces no conscious sensation. But when the mind is moved by a love or desire from within, that is, from the spiritual world, that love reaches out to lay hold of any sense impulses which it spontaneously recognizes as harmonious with itself, and thus as giving pleasure. It focuses the mind upon such sense impulses, drawing them out from the confused background of unconscious sensations, and forming from them a mental picture, an ideal, a promise of achievement for which to strive. Such an ideal may be retained in the memory and recalled long after it has been superseded by other sensations.

In this way the mind, in accord with its active affection or interest, creates its own mental world consisting of those things to which it pays attention, at the same time ignoring or bypassing many sensations that appear irrelevant or of no consequence to its life. Furthermore, the love spontaneously seeks to impose its ideal upon the material environment, to make it actual by bringing all things in the environment into accord with it. Here is where the fixed surroundings play a vital role. They do not readily yield to the demands of the love. Their resistance compels man to search, to investigate, to struggle in the attempt to achieve what his love envisages. Only partially can they be adapted to that ideal. In large measure they prove to be intractable, and the ideal must be modified accordingly. Seldom if ever does one find the actual accomplishment of an objective fully satisfying. To some degree the goal may be changed, the imagined purpose altered by external necessity. And because ideals are born of ignorance or of insufficient knowledge, one may grow more intelligent and wiser by experience. By the insistent requirements of a fixed environment man may learn to obey the laws of Divine order, all of which are inscribed from creation upon the objects and the forces of nature.

Love does not arise within the human mind. It comes from spirits and angels in the other world with whom a man is associated. Any love that is active in the mind produces reflection, determines what a man shall seek and what he shall avoid and therefore what shall form the field of his consciousness. It would appear, therefore, as if man has no mind of his own but is merely swept along by whatever love inspires him. Yet this does not follow, because man can be moved by many different affections at different times. While he is under the influence of one love, he can still remember others that have moved him in the past. Among these memories he may choose one, and by an act of will he may focus his attention upon the objects associated with it.

Reflecting upon such objects opens the gate of influx from these spirits or angels who find in such objects an ideal or goal of accomplishment. Because of this, man can control the spirits who shall influence him. He can attract certain spirits and force others to withdraw. This also is possible because of a fixed environment. Man can purposely turn his attention from one thing to another, and so doing can determine what spirits shall influence his mind. The ability to do this is the source of all human freedom, and yet it often appears as a cause of bondage. We are confronted by immediate and imperative needs that compel us to shift our attention. There are times for work and times for rest. There is hunger that demands attention for the sustenance of the body. There are obligations to others that must be taken care of at specific times, dates to be kept, crucial circumstances to be met that cannot be delayed. Indeed, man's life is made up of constant interruptions that may be very annoying but that cannot be avoided. For this reason man is constantly being forced to pay attention to other things, to break his line of thought, and so to drive away certain spirits and invite others to influence him. Too long a concentration upon one thing leads to weariness and at last to utter inability to think and act. This is the great need for a change of occupation, a vacation, by which to renew one powers of perception and understanding. By means of necessities the Divine Providence leads us whither we would not go. New influences from the other world, and new opportunities resulting, open up vistas of inspiration and insight we could not have foreseen. Yet within the framework of all these necessities, man has the freedom and the responsibility to determine what he will love most of all, what he will repeatedly come back to despite all interruptions.

We see therefore that while the first condition of life on earth, namely, the covering of a material body, places a restriction upon our power of reflection and one which appears to be a serious disadvantage when compared to the life after death, the second condition gives us what appears as a marvelous advantage over spirits and angels, in that by means of a fixed environment we are able to control the affections and loves that shall dominate our life. By turning from one thing to another, by focusing attention upon different objects in nature, we can choose to be inspired either by a good or an evil love and can continually perfect our love and perception of what is good and true. However, once a man has chosen his ruling love and has so far confirmed it that he has no desire to change it, the fixed environment is no longer of any use to him. When this point is reached, the Lord calls him into the spiritual world where each one may be free to develop his chosen love without limit, unless he seeks to injure or destroy the life of others whom the Lord, in His mercy, must protect.

THE IMPORTANCE OF VARIED
HUMAN ASSOCIATIONS

L ife in the natural world differs from life in the spiritual world in that men are brought inevitably into contact and association with all kinds of people. By family relationship, the neighborhood in which one lives, through travel, through social activities, through business and employment, the path of each one is continually crossing the paths of others. Such contacts may be casual and fleeting, but under the influence of mutual interests or common needs the life of one may become closely intertwined with the lives of others, and this perhaps for many years. This is true irrespective of mental states, and it may bind together externally people of extremely diverse forms of mind, disposition, or temperament. From this arises a conflict of wills that may cause suffering varying from a mere momentary irritation to prolonged and severe distress of mind. Such an interplay of heterogeneous natures results from the fact that human society on earth is founded not upon congeniality of spirit but rather upon common needs of the body and of the material world. The uses that bind men together may be performed by the evil as well as by the good. They may be performed from love to the Lord and charity toward the neighbor or from the loves of self and the world. Not only this, but in all men evil tendencies and good tendencies exist side by side. At times they act from one, and at other times from the other. So mixed are the motives that prompt men to action, and so deeply are they concealed, that no one can know with certainty whether he acts from charity or from some selfish ambition.

Conditions under which opposing affections are brought together and held in close association are not confined to individuals of an alien race or nationality, but frequently obtain among members of the same family. Such may have many interests in common and may be bound by strong ties of affection. They may be held together by mutual responsibilities even though they may be poles apart as to ideals of life or principles of action and thus may be incapable of deep mutual sympathy or understanding.

In the other life this is not so. There all consociations are according to affinities of love and affection. Diversity of love spontaneously causes separation, while affinity brings presence. There are no external needs such as exist on earth to compel the association of alien spirits. The only needs that obtain after death are spiritual. The uses performed for one another are all spiritual. It is in accord with these spiritual uses that society there is organized. We read in *Arcana Coelestia* 2449:

> Such is the communication in the other life of all ideas of thought and of all affections, that goods are communicated among the good, and evils among the evil . . . Unless the good and the evil were separated, countless mischiefs would result, and moreover, all association together would be impossible . . . yet all things are most exquisitely consociated, in the heavens according to all the differences of love to the Lord and . . . mutual love, and of the derivative faith; and in the hells according to all the differences of cupidities and of the derivative phantasies. Be it known, however, that the separation is not entire removal, for from no one is what he has had altogether taken away.

All who possess similar affections are, in general, together in one place, in one heaven, and in one society of heaven. So also the particular varieties of one homogeneous society are arranged according to more particular likenesses of affection, of thought, and of use. Thus in heaven the only bonds are those of love, and only those who possess a mutuality of love can be together in the same heaven, the same society, the same house. So also in the hells, those in similar loves of evil are associated and this more closely as their loves are more nearly alike. In heaven the bond is one of mutual love and use, while in hell the bond is one of the need to enlist the cooperation of others for the sake of one's own personal ambition.

Between heaven and hell, therefore, there is "a great gulf fixed" (Luke 16:26). Those from heaven cannot pass over to those in hell, and evil spirits cannot invade the heavens. Those who are spiritually incompatible do not meet, and remain quite unaware of one another. That is because there are no external necessities compelling them to associate. This is not the case in the world of spirits, into which intermediate world every one comes immediately after death. There, for a time, the good and the evil are together very much as they were on earth. Yet, even there, spirits are not bound together by external necessities but solely by loves and interests they have in common. Every one entering that world, unless he has been fully regenerated on earth, carries with him opposing affections by which he is brought into contact with spirits of opposing character. Each one is led by his affections to seek consociation with others of like disposition. Those who have been striving for regeneration retain many habits of thought and life, many appearances and fallacies which they mistake for the truth, and many hereditary tendencies to evil which they have not yet overcome. The converse also is true; namely, that the evil possess acquired habits of use, of charity, and of piety whereby they have adapted their external lives to the demands of society. The purpose of a temporary period of life in the world of spirits is that through a series of experiences and by instruction, mistaken ideas may be corrected and evil habits may be rejected in favor of uses in accord with one's ruling love. And on the contrary, outward pretenses of good and truth may be removed that the inner character of evil may become apparent. By this means the good are gradually separated from the evil, the good being instructed and elevated into heaven, while the evil seek association with their own kind in hell.

This process may at times require a considerable period and may be accompanied by severe temptation and suffering. But at last each one is brought by his own will, through Divine leading, into his place, either in heaven or in hell.

The conditions existing on earth are of the Divine Providence because only by the mingling of people of different characteristics can any one learn to know himself. Only thus can one recognize the quality of evil tendencies in himself and determine to oppose them. No one living in a mutual admiration society could realize his own shortcomings. His pride would be continually fed by the praise and approbation of others. But when he is in contact with opposing natures, he is given the constant opportunity to reflect upon his own affections, to judge them, and select those which he wishes to cultivate while rejecting those he finds objectionable. Especially in periods of spiritual decline, when evil conditions are tolerated in human society and when the dominant loves are those of self and the world, many are bound together by external bonds who are interiorly very diverse. Families are forced to live together in single rooms or in close quarters that bring them into continual conflict with one another. They may have to live in neighborhoods largely occupied by criminals. They may be restricted in association by conditions of war or of political and social antagonisms. Nevertheless, even on earth all men have a longing to associate with others who understand them and sympathize with their aims and purposes. A most important need is felt for a home where one's own family may enjoy privacy and a sense of freedom from outside pressures. Human nature, even on earth, causes all men constantly to seek congenial companionship and to struggle against the conditions that throw them together with those who are antagonistic and unresponsive.

What is of particular interest to us at the moment is that the difference between conditions on earth and corresponding conditions in the spiritual world is due to a difference in the power of reflection. On earth men are compelled to reflect upon bodily needs and worldly desires with their resultant uses. They are brought into association with others by limitations of time and place and opportunity, by the lack of economic means, or by considerations of health, of employment or business. Such restraints often appear as unfortunate or even cruel, and yet no one can altogether avoid them. The truth is that without them no one could regenerate. Only by such a mingling of divergent natures can one be led to perceive the quality of his own states of mind. Without some such compulsion no one would reflect upon his inner thoughts and emotions. Every one takes these for granted and accepts them at face value unless his judgment of them is challenged. Reflection first arises when one sees these same qualities in others and notes their effect upon himself. Not otherwise can any one overcome the bias or prejudice with which he is wont to judge himself. Concerning this we read:

> When [a] man does not reflect upon those things that are in his mind or . . . [spirit,] namely, how he thinks, what he thinks, what he does, and whence he acts [he has no knowledge of these things] . . . Without reflection he knows nothing, except that a thing is . . . [He does not know] its quality. But if he reflects in himself from others, or if he suffers others to reflect upon him, and to say of what quality he is, then . . . [first] he can know that he is of such a quality. Otherwise he can never know it, but he remains in his phantasies, and from them he reflects upon others. (SE 734).

This is a matter of universal experience, and it is permitted by the Lord in order that man may learn to know himself, to judge as to the quality of his habitual thoughts and feelings. Judgment requires knowledge, and without knowledge there can be no freedom of choice. The whole purpose of man's life on earth is that he may learn to judge between good and evil, truth and falsity, and may freely choose the one and reject the other. To this end he is compelled by circumstances to mingle with people of alien character and given the opportunity to reflect upon his own innate tendencies. Even given the opportunity, there is no assurance that a man will avail himself of it. To do so requires an act of will and a struggle, for every one is prone to reflect upon others rather than upon himself. Every one naturally assumes that he is right and that those who disagree with him are wrong. The temptation to judge others harshly and one's self with great leniency is very strong. This is especially true if one has no standard of judgment based on Divine revelation and no religious conscience from which to judge.

However, so far as regeneration has been achieved, this same kind of struggle and temptation is no longer necessary. The judgment has been made, and whatever is contrary to the laws of love and charity is rejected at once, spontaneously, and with effort. Close association with alien spirits becomes a hindrance rather than a help, and then the Lord provides that one may enter the spiritual world where he may enjoy the association only of such as are congenial spirits. Further growth is effected not by conflict with the evil but by a continual perfection of the good. This is achieved by association with others in the promotion of uses mutually loved, receiving from others new affections and new thoughts whereby the mind of each one is enriched and perfected. Such is the kingdom of heaven.

REFLECTION IN THE SPIRITUAL WORLD IS ON QUALITIES OF LOVE, WISDOM, AND USE

It has been pointed out that both men on earth and spirits after death really live in both worlds at the same time. Every one must receive sense impulses from the world of nature and affections of love from the spiritual world, both of these being necessary to produce consciousness. While man is on earth, although he has all the organs of sensation and is in constant touch with the objects in his environment from which a stream of sense impulses pours in upon his mind during every waking moment, nevertheless no conscious realization of his surroundings will result unless he is being stirred at the same time by some affection, some interest, some desire that causes him to focus his attention and so to notice a particular set of sense impulses. On the other hand, although every one is surrounded by spirits and angels, they cannot produce any conscious effect upon the mind unless there is a stream of sense impulses knocking upon the door of consciousness. If one were deaf, blind, and incapable of taste, smell, or touch, even if he were alive, he would have no love, no emotion, no desire, and therefore no reflection that could produce consciousness.

It follows from this that men on earth must receive some influx from the spiritual world, and spirits after death must receive some impulse from the world of nature in order to enjoy any conscious life whatever. This must be true in spite of the fact that while on earth men are completely unaware of their spiritual associates, and spirits after death are wholly unconscious of the material world. On earth we feel affections or loves as if they arose in our minds and have no knowledge of whence they come. So also spirits in the other world are moved by the ideas present in the minds of men on earth but perceive these as if they originated in themselves and remain wholly ignorant of their source.

Ideas formed in the imagination are all derived from the physical senses, but they have been so ordered as to clothe, represent, and make tangible some love or affection. They have been separated from the material properties of matter to produce ideals. These ideal forms are what affect and move the minds of spirits and angels, performing for them the same function as the direct touch with nature performs for men on earth. For this reason it is said that the whole spiritual world rests upon mankind as a common basis. It is solely because they are touched and moved by a constant stream of impulses originating in the world of nature, but elevated thence to the plane of the imagination, that spirits are capable of reflection and therefore of consciousness.

Nevertheless, the fact that in the other life no one possesses his own bodily sense organs produces a profound difference in the kind of reflection that is possible. Concerning this we read:

> The state of spirits relatively to the state of men appears similar at first glance, but yet it differs greatly. They think, indeed, similarly, and will similarly, but they are different as to reflections. (*SE* 4716)

> After death, reflection upon inconveniences and punishments is taken away from man; for external bonds are removed and the man is left to his own disposition, thus to the delights of his life, so that he may act according to them. For in the other life a reflection other than prevails during the life of the body is requisite. In this there is reflection upon honors, gains, reputation, dangers to life and the like. These things are taken away, and the spirit is left to his own disposition which he had acquired to himself in the life of the body. (*SE* 4756)

The difference between the two worlds is caused by the different plane upon which reflection takes place. As long as one lives in the body he is aware of the source from which sense impulses come, but he is not aware of the source whence spiritual influences come. Therefore attention is fixed upon material objects and the mechanical forces in our natural environment. Even when we picture these things in our imagination, we notice their material attributes and characteristics such as size, shape, weight, color, texture. We are interested in these things because of the physical needs they fill and the worldly uses they perform. Because of this we are said to live in a natural world which is characterized by these properties and uses. At the same time we feel affection, emotion, desire, and we can perceive in some degree the qualities of these spiritual things, but only as they exist in ourselves, wherefore we call them "human qualities"—thoughts, abstract ideas, and spiritual or moral aspirations.

After death it is altogether otherwise. Then one is no longer affected by material things directly, but only after they have been idealized in the minds of men on earth. Ideals are representative of things immaterial and supernatural. These representations are perceived by spirits in the other world without realizing whence they come. But spirits are conscious of one another and of their spiritual environment. They are aware of spiritual things as existing outside of themselves and as constituting a world to be sensed, explored, and enjoyed. This is the living world of the Divine Proceeding, the world of Divine Love and Divine Wisdom accommodated to human reception. Yet these spiritual objects and forces are perceived in forms altogether similar to those found in nature, because they can become visible to us under no other form or aspect than what has been impressed upon the external senses during life on earth. To create such representative forms is the Divine purpose in providing a material world of objects. Not by any other means can spiritual things become visible and tangible. For this reason no one can be created in the spiritual world but must first live on earth in a body sensitive to material things.

The difference between reflection on earth and reflection in the spiritual world is further explained, as follows:

Man in the world reflects from his corporeal memory . . .
When a man sees another, he reflects upon all that he had heard
and has experienced concerning the person; and [he] acknowledges him as [a] friend and companion with whom he has associated and [has] for various reasons, entered into friendship. But not
so spirits. They acknowledge as [a] friend him who is like themselves; for an acquaintance, every one who receives their ideas; but
this with much variety, and whether they have been acquainted or
not. (*SE* 4716)

From this it is clear that after death every one is brought into
association with those who are in similar loves to his own, and he at
once feels himself to be among friends. It is as if he had known them
always, even though he had never met them before. He does not
reflect upon who they are, where they have lived, or what they have
done during their life on earth. These things would be regarded as
of no consequence because he already perceives the interior quality
of the ones he meets to be in sympathy with his own. There would
be no thought of person from family connection, from social station,
from outward appearance, manners, or dress. He would have regard only to the quality of love which they present in a representative form.

They see each other because an accordant love is roused in the
mind of each one and made visible through the memory of corresponding forms derived originally either from their own experience
on earth or from ideas in the minds of men still living in the natural
world. Whence these memories or impulses come is not known, nor
is it reflected upon. Only the results of it are consciously enjoyed as
if originating in themselves, while the attention is focused solely
upon the spiritual things that come into view. Spirits live in a world
of human affections and human thoughts made tangible in
correspondential forms derived, in the last analysis, from physical
sensation. Thus from their own memory of past experience, or from
the memory of men still living on earth, spirits derive the forms, the
mental pictures through which spiritual things are seen and felt.

For this reason, all the appearances in the spiritual world are similar to the forms existing in nature. Houses, garments, trees, plants, fields, rivers, mountains—all of these appear similar to those on earth. Yet to the spirits they are merely the medium whereby they sense and feel loves, or goods, and truths. Spirits pay little attention to the forms, being delighted with the spiritual realities of which the forms are but clothing. Such appearances are not subject to the restriction of space and time, nor are they regarded as to any material properties. The appearances may change suddenly. They may appear and disappear, but the spirits do not reflect upon such changes and find nothing strange or surprising about them. They seem perfectly natural because the plane of reflection is not upon the forms but upon the spiritual things they represent. The forms change as the states of the spirits change, not because the spiritual things really change, but only the way the spirits are affected by them, how they look at them, from what point of view they regard them. In explanation, the number quoted from the *Spiritual Experiences* continues:

> Man reflects upon the various things wherewith he may array, and with which he does array himself; and this variously . . . [Spirits do not do this.] Garments are given them according to their state. They do not know whence and at what time; nor do they care. Man knows of what sort is his house, his rooms, his halls, and many things, also the furniture. Spirits, indeed, are similarly circumstanced; but when their surroundings are changed, when new things are given them, when they are provided with furniture, they rarely reflect [upon] from whence, or when, these things came. But it is different with one spirit to what it is with another. Likewise, when he comes into another place he does not know where he had been before, [and] thus does not turn back from the former to the latter, as does man. In a word, reflections are circumstanced according to the states in which they are . . . [whether in the other life or] in the world. In respect to reflections, so many things occur that they cannot be described . . . Still . . .

[spirits] have a wakefulness and life . . . [which], on account of the difference of reflections . . . differs greatly . . . from the wakefulness and life of man . . . The angels think and act in a far more excellent manner than men [do], although they are not so well acquainted with the state of man as to be able to institute a comparison. The principal cause is that they have no memory of the past as regards such things as are external, but [only] as regards such things as are internal thus which are of faith and eternal life; but . . . whence or how these things are learned, they do not remember. In this they are like infants who learn and know not how.

This teaching may help one to understand why the spiritual world and all things in it appear similar to things in the natural world and yet are altogether different, being wholly spiritual. The forms upon which angels and spirits look are derived from the world of nature, but the things they see, hear, touch, and feel are not material objects, but instead are goods and truths. These goods and truths exist outside the angels. They exist in the Divine of the Lord that "makes heaven." They are divine creations and not figments of man's imagination. They are merely perceived differently according to the changes of state with the angels and spirits.

CONCERNING REFLECTION IN THE
WORLD OF SPIRITS

The phenomena of the spiritual world are innumerable. In variety they far exceed the phenomena of nature; and yet consider how innumerable these are! Those in the spiritual world represent far more perfectly the infinity of God. Yet they are all the product of reflection. Reflection is but the mode by which these phenomena are produced. Therefore, only by exploring the doctrine of reflection is it possible to learn and understand rationally the nature of life in the spiritual world. We shall attempt no more than to trace in brief outline the distinction between reflection as it occurs in the world of spirits and in heaven and in hell.

To begin with we must remember that the spirit that awakes in the spiritual world when the body dies is the same as the mind which had previously lived in the body. The phenomena of the spiritual world, therefore, are the same as the phenomena of mental life on earth. Wonderful, strange, and seemingly fantastic as are many of the appearances of the spiritual world as described in the Writings, they all are governed by the same laws as those which control the operation of the mind. If we could remove our attention from the properties and characteristics of material things and focus our thought instead entirely upon things of love and faith on which truly human values depend, we could form some idea of what the spiritual world is like. It is a world completely human. In it are all those things which we value as human qualities—love, mercy, justice, use and service, worship, knowledge, intelligence, insight, perception, truth—all these set free from the restrictions of a fixed material environment. We perceive these things dimly in our minds as abstractions only, as long as we are in the body. We may know that they exist in God, that they are really outside of ourselves, that they are not mere creations of our imagination; yet we cannot picture them objectively. Nevertheless, there is no phenomenon of the spiritual world of which we may not form some faint but essentially accurate idea by reflecting upon our own mental states. Our idea will be vague and imperfect, however, because we cannot completely remove from our thought the properties of matter, ideas of fixed time and space, which really have no place in the spiritual world.

The truth is, that when we wake up in the spiritual world we will go on thinking and feeling just as we did before. Our thoughts and emotions will seem exactly the same as before. At first we will not be aware of the slightest change. We will seem to be in our accustomed surroundings, in company with those we have known and loved. We will not know that we have departed out of the world. Only by angelic instruction can we be brought to reflect upon our former state of life. But as we do so we begin to notice strange things such as could not happen on earth. By this experience we are brought to recognize that we are indeed in a spiritual world. This reflection must come from our association with others, that is, from angels whose use and function it is to preside over the process of resurrection from the dead. Without such instruction we would continue to believe that we were still on earth. Indeed, with the evil, who presently reject the instruction of the angels, the fantasy that they are still in the body returns, and some never escape from it. It is otherwise with the good who love spiritual things and who are willing to be instructed. They gladly accept the idea that they have departed from the world and eagerly seek to explore the wonders of their new life. Yet after a brief time they no longer reflect upon this but take it for granted, enjoying the spiritual world even as men on earth enjoy the natural world. Swedenborg describes the experience of a newly arrived spirit, saying:

> He knew not at first where he was, supposing himself to be in
> the world altogether as if living in the body, for . . . all souls . . .
> [recently] from the life of the body [have this impression], inas-

much as they are not then gifted with reflection upon place (*SE* 2031) . . . [or upon] time, the objects of the senses, and the like, of which I have spoken elsewhere, and which would enable them to know that they are in another life, only that they live, as it were, in the body, and think accordingly. (*SE* 2032)

That souls lose nothing of the things which they had in the life of the body, you will see everywhere affirmed; thus they neither know nor can know that they are in the other life, but [suppose] that they are in the world, inasmuch as they are without that reflection which is excited by things stored up in the memory; nor is what is in the memory excited except by means of objects, and objects are not presented unless by those who are in society together. Reflection is also given, but by the Lord, that they are in the other life. (*SE* 1903)

Moreover, that without reflection they cannot know that they are in the other life may appear from the nature of reflection, as man does not know the distances of objects without reflecting upon what intervenes, nor can he judge of times but in the same manner. And so of many other things besides; for reflection enables . . . man to know the quality and quantity of anything. (*SE* 1904)

A spirit who spake with me positively affirmed that he did not know otherwise than that he was . . . myself, especially when he did not reflect upon the subject; but my own reflections were that spirits did know themselves to be spirits separate from men. In a word, without reflection they know nothing else, nor is reflection given except with those who converse with them and give responses, and then converse with others also. Reflection is indeed given without the speech of man with spirits, but this is effected by the Lord. (*SE* 1852)

The first state of man after death resembles his state in the world, for he is then likewise in externals, having a like face, like speech, and a like disposition, thus a like civil and moral life; and . . . [consequently] he is made aware that he is not still in the world only by giving attention to what he encounters, and from his having been told by . . . angels when he was resuscitated that he had become a spirit. Thus is one life continued into the other, and death is merely [a] transition. (*HH* 493)

As soon as we realize that we are in the other life, because our thought is focused upon the desires, ambitions, and delights habitual with us, we at once wish to meet friends who have gone before us. We think of these friends just as we did on earth, or as we knew them, especially as to those qualities of mind by which we had become conjoined with them (*SE* 2771; *CL* 273; *HH* 494). We think of things we had in common with them, mutual interests, concordant ideas whereby there had been a meeting of minds and an interchange of affections. Thus we meet them, but there is no reflection upon their physical characteristics, no thought as to their former place of abode, their station in earthly society, or their family relationships.

The meeting takes place on the plane of the natural mind, the animus with its characteristic affections and thoughts. The whole world of spirits is the state in which reflection is focused upon the things of this external mind. For this reason we appear to be in surroundings similar to those we had been familiar with on earth— in the same country, the same city, the same house. We appear to have the same occupation, the same place in society, the same duties and responsibilities. We have the same religious affiliations and seek consociation with others of the same faith. The reason is that we are in the company of the same spirits who had been attendant upon us, without our realizing it, during the life of the body. For this reason they seem to be familiar to us, as if they were friends and companions we had previously known.

At first we do not normally reflect upon the fact that they are not the persons with whom we have been outwardly associated on earth. The realization of this arises only when we begin to reflect that we are no longer on earth but are in the spiritual world. Such reflection is induced by instruction from the angels who at the same time impart a sense that there is no real separation, that we are still present with those we love, that we can continue to serve them and be served by them, and this even more fully than before. Thus the first awakening is accompanied by a far more perfect realization of the Divine Providence and the overruling mercy of the Lord in caring for every essential need of those on earth. For this reason there is no sense of worry and anxiety for the future such as what usually oppresses those on earth at the death of a close friend.

The spontaneous association in the world of spirits of those who are similar as to externals, that is as to the loves and the thoughts of the external mind, causes the formation of imaginary heavens. It causes spirits to congregate into societies of those in similar faiths and similar modes of civil and religious life. The simulation which has been habitually practiced on earth is still possible and is continued as a matter of course. Deeper feelings remain hidden behind an outward appearance of politeness, courtesy, and friendship. Sincerity, justice, honesty, and piety are expressed in speech and action. These appearances are accepted uncritically by those who are simple in heart, and for this reason they will respect and reverence others whether they be interiorly good or evil. Such confiding spirits, therefore, come under the influence of evil spirits who seek to dominate over them. In this respect all in such imaginary heavens are mingled very much as they were on earth.

Before the Last Judgment, such societies could be maintained for a very long time, even for centuries, constantly receiving new additions from the world and therefore growing continually in numbers and in power. The larger they grew the greater their influence over the minds of men on earth, specially through the weight of tradition. They tended to hold the minds of men bound to the beliefs, the ideas, and the modes of life which had been accepted as Divinely commanded. Nor could this bondage be broken except by the Lord Himself. He alone had power to penetrate the appearances, the fallacies, and the evil practices to which they led, and this by opening, at His Second Advent, the internal sense of the Word. As this was done, the mask of pretense could be removed and the true character of the evil could be made manifest, whereupon their power over the good spirits was broken, and a separation could take place between the good and the evil. Since the Last Judgment, at the time of the Lord's Second Coming, although such temporary associations are still being formed in the world of spirits, they can be judged periodically, and cannot be maintained for a period longer than twenty or thirty years. Such is the liberation that has been effected by the Lord through the giving of the Heavenly Doctrine. For this reason there is no need for the Lord to come again, and the New Church, which He is now establishing on earth and in the heavens, will be eternal.

What is here described was true of the simple who could be innocently deceived by the evil and held under their authority. But those who belonged to the Primitive Christian Church—when the Lord Jesus Christ was worshiped as God, and before the meaning of the Gospels had been perverted by false doctrines—could not be held in the imaginary heavens. They were instructed by angels and introduced into heavenly societies. They could reflect upon the teaching of the Word and steadily progress into an ever truer understanding of it and into a more perfect life of love to the Lord and charity. They could be formed into genuine societies of heaven, into which, after the Judgment, the simple good spirits could be introduced. Those who belonged to these heavenly societies could be given a part in the Lord's work of redemption. They could assist in breaking up the imaginary heavens and liberating those "under the altar" who had been held bound there. Such, we believe, are included among those "twelve apostles who had followed the Lord during His life on earth, and who were sent on the 19th of June 1770, to proclaim throughout the whole spiritual world the Gospel that the Lord God Jesus Christ reigns as the one God of heaven and earth."

What we wish to emphasize is that all this is effected solely by means of reflection induced from without by instruction and experience. For reflection, knowledge is necessary, in the spiritual world as well as on earth. The Lord had to come, He had to give His Word, and this had to be written simultaneously in both worlds. It was the internal sense of the Word revealed, and the doctrines of the New Church made known, that alone could break the hold of the evil upon the good. It was by learning this truth and reflecting upon it that the false assumptions of the former churches were recognized for what they were, and so repudiated. In the spiritual world, however, this great change could take place quickly, while on earth it requires many centuries. The reason is that in the spiritual world there are no fixed conditions of time and space, no binding requirement of physical needs, and the mind is free to follow where the inner love would lead. We are told that the Last Judgment was effected in the world of spirits in the course of a single year, 1757, and it has been slowly progressing here on earth ever since and promises to continue almost imperceptibly for many generations to come.

REFLECTION IN THE FINAL STATE
AFTER DEATH:
THE CASE WITH INFANTS WHO DIE

Passing from the world of spirits to a final home, either in heaven or in hell, is like passing from the natural world into the spiritual world—at least in this respect, that it is effected by a change in the plane of reflection. While man is on earth he cannot reflect apart from ideas of time, space, and matter. He can conceive of spiritual things only as abstractions. He cannot think of them objectively without ascribing to them the properties of nature. He is held in this mode of thinking not only because of the body through which all sensation must pass to reach his mind but also because of the pressing needs, responsibilities, and restrictions of the world in which he lives. Only occasionally, and for brief periods, can one withdraw himself from these limitations and by a conscious effort focus attention upon spiritual things. This requires an effort that cannot be long sustained. Nor is it possible for him even then to remove completely the idea of space and time.

When the body dies these external bonds are removed, and one can begin to reflect apart from them. Nevertheless, everyone has both an external mind and an internal mind. The external mind is active in the presence, and under the influence, of others; and the internal mind can become consciously awake only when one is spiritually alone. When man first awakes in the spiritual world, he is separated from all things of the body and its earthly environment; but he is still in contact with other spirits in whose presence he feels and thinks from the external mind. This mind has been adjusted to society. It has been trained in the forms of politeness and courtesy and has learned to conform to the customs and ideas of those with whom one is associated. As a result, even in the spiritual world, a man at first thinks and wills, speaks and acts, from the external mind when in the presence of other spirits who have similar externals. By gradual stages, however, he seeks to express his inner feelings and beliefs. He is attracted to others who are interiorly in sympathy with him. The real joy of his life consists in the expression of these things, and every one is led by experiences through which he passes to reflect upon these inner feelings, to become aware of them, and to try to ultimate them in speech and action.

It is of providence that even spirits may be able to conceal the affections of the internal mind, not only when they are evil, but also when they are good. He must be able to conceal them when they are evil in order that he may gain the approbation of others and their assistance in the achievement of his personal ambitions. But he must be able to conceal them when they are good in order to protect them from injury by others who are opposed to them. There must therefore be degrees of friendship. There must be some with whom a man may associate externally and temporarily for the sake of cooperation in a common use or mutual enterprise. There must be others who can share their deeper feelings with mutual understanding and confidence. And there must be some who can freely bare their inmost loves and thoughts to each other without fear or restraint. But every one has the need for privacy—the privacy of thought and affection, of the home, and of each individual life even within the home. Such privacy exists, we are told, even with the celestial angels. Only husband and wife can be together in the inner recesses of the home. Children and close friends may be together with them in the outer courts of the home. Companions and fellow workers may be together in the same society, and there may be contact with others, even with those in hell for some specific purpose or to perform some special service. But in this case they are clothed in official garments that protect against the violation of the precious things within their hearts and minds.

When one first enters the spiritual world there are, except in very rare cases, many things in the external mind that are out of harmony with the internal mind. During one's sojourn in the world of spirits these disharmonies are gradually brought to light. As one reflects more and more upon one's inner states, the discrepancy becomes apparent, and one feels an increasing urge to remove what is contrary to his inmost love. The opposition between the two becomes evident by contact with others that causes one to reflect upon one's deeper feelings. Gradually one learns to reflect more often and more persistently, and by degrees such reflection becomes easier, more natural and more delightful, until it becomes a second nature, and one lives altogether in the internal mind. As this change takes place, one draws near to one's permanent spiritual home.

The state that is characteristic of both heaven and hell is one in which one normally and habitually reflects upon the internal mind and finds in this a sense of peace, of satisfaction, and of happiness that is not otherwise possible. It is a state of freedom, of feeling at home as among family and friends, and there one wills to stay, feeling under no obligation to go elsewhere. It is a permanent abode that is freely chosen. It is a place where one can think most clearly, act most spontaneously, and express his deepest loves most perfectly. It is therefore where man can perform his individual use to others most fully, and in doing so can feel the greatest delight and happiness. That is the case in heaven because the greatest joy of the angels is to serve others, and through them, to serve the Lord.

In hell, however, the case is quite different. When one's inmost love is evil, one finds satisfaction only in dominating over others, in taking for one's own the goods of others, and finding one's own pleasure in bringing suffering upon others. Evil spirits are brought together and are held together by these mutual antagonisms which find no fulfillment except in so far as they can be exercised against others. Hell, therefore, is a perpetual clash of opposing wills, a constant warfare, with all its cruelty and hatred. Such evil passions are continually restrained by the laws of the Divine Providence for the protection of the good. They are permitted so far as they may be of use to check the evils of others, to bring punishment upon them and so deter them from worse evils, or to balance one force of evil against another. There is no love of use in hell. There is only the love of gain and of dominion for the sake of which one may work very

hard only to be confronted with failure, disappointment, and disil-
lusion, because one's real love can never be satisfied. Nevertheless,
even in hell, use is the only thing that can sustain human life. The
evil spirits discover that they must perform some use in order to
secure what to them are the necessities of life—food, clothing, and
habitation. These are all given freely to the angels, but in hell they
cannot be secured without making some useful return. For this
reason evil spirits perform in hell something of the use they would
have performed gladly and with great joy had they been willing to
receive love to the Lord and charity into their hearts. This is the only
use of which they are capable. But in hell they are compelled to
perform it reluctantly, and in doing so they feel no happiness but
only a constant desire to exercise their malevolent ambition to bring
injury to others.

However, evil spirits are reduced to a willingness to perform a
use when they have been deterred by the fear of punishment from
doing the evil things they love. Then their evil passions are for the
time being laid to rest, and by concentration upon some work their
external mind is brought into order, and they sense the nearest thing
to contentment that is possible to them. The fear of punishment is
temporarily in abeyance, and their evil loves do not break forth but
merely smolder beneath the surface. Thus the Lord brings the hells
into order and under obedience to His Divine will. Yet He cannot
take away completely all their sense of freedom without destroying
their life. He must permit the hope of achieving their evil ends to
survive even when they see no immediate possibility of success. He
must protect their freedom and give it free rein just so far as to do so
may be turned to some good of which the evil spirits can have no
idea. But beyond this point it must be strictly restrained, and herein
lies the frustration that is the eternal lot of the wicked.

Just the opposite is the case in heaven. When one's inmost love
is good, and when one's greatest delight is to serve others and to
promote their happiness, there is no need for Divine restriction.
When those who have this love in common are associated together,
each one can achieve his highest ambition and at the same time

assist others to attain theirs. The success of one does not bring with it the failure of another. What one gains does not mean a loss to another. Each one performs his use with no thought of personal reward, feeling his happiness in the happiness of others. Such is the state of peace and joy which it is the Lord's will to impart to all men. This is the very heaven for the sake of which the entire universe was created. This end of the Divine Providence is achieved in spite of man's unwillingness to receive it. For those who refuse it, the Lord provides a hell where they may still enjoy some measure of life even if the delights thereof are evil. And in His mercy, between heaven and hell there is "a great gulf fixed" to prevent the evil from destroying or even impairing the happiness of the good.

Just a brief word about the case of those who die in infancy. There have been two opposite ideas about this. Some have questioned the Divine justice by holding that infants who die are preferred above all others, since they attain the joys of heaven without sustaining all the toil and temptation incident to adult life on earth. Why should the rest of us be subjected to this great hardship when the ultimate goal could have been assured so easily? Others have held that the Lord is unjust because He has deprived the infants who die of all the advantages that accrue to those who endure the burden of life and the challenge of temptation. It is thought that the infants can never perform so high a use because they lack the knowledge, the training, and the experience by which alone wisdom may be achieved. Both ideas are wrong. Every one, we are taught, is taken into the spiritual world at the time that is best for his eternal welfare and at the same time is best for others. The Lord alone knows for what eternal use in heaven each one is created. He knows what earthly preparation for that use is necessary. He knows when that preparation has been completed and when a longer sojourn on earth would prove to be detrimental to one's eternal happiness instead of beneficial. There are uses in the Grand Man of heaven that can be performed only by those who have died in infancy. They are uses that require a degree of innocence that could not be preserved through the struggles of adult life. It is true that the infant will lack an individual fund of knowledge and experience that can be acquired only through a lifetime of effort, but he will not be limited by this, because he can learn from others. After all, the difference between an infant and an adult in this respect is not so great as might appear. For if we consider, we may realize that what any one attains by his own investigation and experience is very little compared to all that he has acquired from others through instruction, conversation, and reading. Infants raised in heaven can become wise, even to the celestial degree, although they have had scarcely any personal experience on earth. However, the use they can perform in heaven will differ from one which requires a store of individual knowledge and the struggle to overcome on earth the evil tendencies of the proprium. Such a one also may become wise, even to the celestial degree. But he will have something of great value to give to others which the infant lacks. The use of each may be just as great, but it will be distinctively different in kind. And in each case it could be provided for only by the Providence that fixed the moment of death at the time appointed by the Lord in His infinite wisdom. "He that is our God is the God of salvation; and unto God the Lord belong the issues . . . of death" (Psalm 68:20).

REFLECTION UPON THE WORD

We have pointed out that only by means of a fixed environment can man be led to reflect upon his own affections and
thoughts, and thus realize their quality. Unless he does so he cannot
know what they are. Taking them for granted without reflection, he
has no desire to change them. There must be something outside of
man, something that is independent of his shifting states and moods,
which he may use as a fulcrum to draw himself out of one state and
into another by an act of will. Just as the body can be transported
from one place to another by walking only because the ground is
immovable; just as man can lift himself off of the ground only by
leaping, or propelling his body against a resisting surface, or by
taking hold of something stationary above him and pulling himself
up by his arms; just as a boat can be moved through the water by
oars or propellers only because the water resists the pressure; or as
an airplane can be moved through the air by similar means, or
propelled by rockets; so also it is with the progress of the mind. No
one can purposely change the state of his mind without appealing to
something stationary outside of the mind itself.

The entire environment of the natural world is such an immovable fulcrum. Its objects, with their distinct qualities, are fixed. If
they are changed, it is by means of forces that are independent of
man's mind. Thus there are facts and laws that man may learn to
understand and that he may use to achieve his progress. By seizing
upon these stable things man can change his ideas, his opinions, and
his objectives, and the tool by which he lays hold of them is what is
called "reflection." One may observe these fixed ultimates at different times, in different states of mind, and from different points of
view, and so doing he can become aware of his own changing states.
He can analyze them, appraise them, and judge their quality in
relation to his life.

Such reflection upon the objects and forces of nature enables man to change the states of his external mind, but this by itself cannot empower him to change the states of his internal mind. The external mind has to do with man's relation to the world of nature, with the needs of the body, and with external pleasures and worldly ambitions. The internal mind, on the other hand, is concerned with spiritual states, with man's relation to the Lord, to the Word, and to the laws of the spiritual world. These cannot be learned from nature. They have to do with things invisible and intangible to the bodily senses. They cannot be learned by sense-experience but solely from what the Lord says by means of Divine revelation. This must come by way of the bodily senses through reading and hearing the Word which, for this purpose, serves as a fixed ultimate by which to become aware of spiritual states of mind, and their quality. Concerning this we are taught:

> Without the Word no one would possess spiritual intelligence, which consists in having [a] knowledge of . . . God, of heaven and hell, and of a life after death; nor would [he] know anything whatever about the Lord, about faith in Him . . . nor anything about redemption, by means of which nevertheless comes salvation. (SS 114)

The knowledge that there are spiritual things existing in a world outside of man and remaining constant irrespective of man's changing state of mind is vital to any spiritual progression. There must be a love that is universal, eternal, and the same for all men. There must be laws, principles, truths that are constant, unchanging, and absolute. Unless this were so there would be no criterion from which to judge one's own ever shifting states of affection, of thought, and of opinion. Unless this were so, no one could possibly know the quality of his own thoughts and feelings in order that he might judge them, alter them, and improve them. He would take for granted whatever he might feel spontaneously to be true and good and would never question it. No one can be led to reflect upon these deeper things that belong to the internal mind except by means of the Word. As we read:

> It may also be stated that the doctrine of faith effects nothing whatever with man except the Lord gives him to reflect. Wherefore men learn what is true and good from the Lord's Word in order that they may thereby reflect upon themselves [and judge] whether they are such (as the Word teaches they ought to be). This reflection is awakened in them at certain times, especially in times of trouble. Wherefore, to know truth is of the greatest moment; [for] without the knowledges of truths there can be no reflection, and consequently no reformation. (*SE* 737)

The whole purpose of the Word is to teach man what is true in the sight of the Lord. It is to teach him the laws that govern the life of the internal mind, the laws that obtain in the spiritual world into which all men will come after the body dies and after the fixed laws and objects of nature have been left behind. Spiritual truths, the laws of the spiritual world, are independent of any human mind. They are eternal, unchanging and universal. They exist in the Divine proceeding, that is, in the Divine of the Lord which we are told "makes heaven." They are therefore a fulcrum by means of which man may deliberately change his own inner feelings of affection and his own ideas of human life and happiness. They are the sole means whereby man may progress spiritually into ever greater intelligence and wisdom and may acquire loves, affections, and ends more nearly in accord with those of the Lord and His heavenly kingdom.

Because there is one God, the Creator and Preserver of the entire universe, there is one Divine truth, one Divine law that applies to all men, in all time, and in every earth in the starry heaven. The Lord has appeared to men everywhere and has spoken this Word in accommodation to man's ability to understand in every age from the beginning of time. He spoke it to those of the Most Ancient Church, to Noah and the prophets of the Ancient Church, to Abram and Moses, and the prophets of the Old Testament. He spoke it immediately to His disciples while He was on earth, and through the Gospels His teaching was preserved for all the generations of Christians after His resurrection. And at His Second Advent he has spoken it as adapted to man's rational understanding in the Heavenly Doctrine of the New Jerusalem. Whenever the true knowledge of God and of religion was threatened with destruction, the Lord has come to reveal it anew that men might always be able to advance from spiritual ignorance to knowledge, intelligence, and wisdom, and this by reflecting upon what is true in itself, what is transcendent over the appearances, fallacies, and opinions of erring human minds.

Now the Word is unique in this: although it comes to man through the bodily senses—just as do all the other objects of nature—it enables one to penetrate the appearances of nature and opens to view things spiritual, things intangible to the bodily senses. It is so written as to contain within the obvious sense of the letter untold depths of meaning, to the discovery of which man may be led by his innate love of learning. The human mind is created to perceive spiritual truth. The delight of understanding is instilled in him by the Lord from earliest infancy, and this delight knows no boundary, but leads the mind on, even to the source of all truth, the first cause and origin of all things, and thus to a knowledge of God. Through the Word the love of spiritual knowledge and understanding is roused, and man is inspired to seek it, and to cherish it and choose it above the loves of self and of the world. It is therefore the sole medium of spiritual growth and progress even during man's life on earth. It continues to be the only fulcrum for the perfection of man's spiritual life after the fixed ultimates of nature have been left behind.

We are told, therefore, that the Word is written in both worlds. It appears in heaven in written form that is stable and unchanging. Unlike the other appearances that surround the angels, it does not change with their shifting states. It remains there as a fixed ultimate, outside the angels, and performs a service similar to what was previously performed by the fixed ultimates of nature. In order that the Word might be written on earth, it had to be written at the same time in heaven. "Inasmuch," we read, "as the Divine truth passed down through the heavens even to the world, it became adapted to [the] angels in heaven, and also to men in the world" (*TCR* 85). That it continues to exist there as a fixed ultimate, unlike all other spiritual appearances, is clear from what is said in the *Doctrine of the Sacred Scripture* 72:

> In every large Society of heaven a copy of the Word, written by angels inspired by the Lord, is kept in its sanctuary, lest being elsewhere, it should be altered in some point.

We are also told that there are two different kinds of writing in heaven, one "that exists without the aid of the hand, from mere correspondences with the thoughts . . . [and another written by the hand. The latter alone is said to be] permanent" (*HH* 262). So it is in heaven as it is on earth: there are books written by men expressing human thoughts and ideas that reflect the degree of knowledge and intelligence of the author. And there is the Word, written by the Lord, conveying the eternal truths that could be fully compassed by no finite mind, and yet which men may grasp partially, and with increasing fullness and perfection to all eternity. So it is said in the *Apocalypse Revealed* 200:

> All thought, speech and writing derive its essence and life from him who thinks, speaks and writes. The man with his quality is therein; but the Lord alone is in the Word.

The Word, therefore, as it exists in heaven, is the sole medium whereby spirits and angels can progress spiritually, and this by reflecting upon what the Word teaches and learning thereby how to change the states of the internal mind and grow in the understanding and life of the Divine and eternal laws therein revealed.